Jobs for Tib

By Debbie Croft

T0360168

Tib is sad.

Tib can not get big jobs.

Tib can not dig.

Tib can tug.

But Tib did a job for Dan.

Gus the bus was in the mud!

Tib got in the mud.

Gus is **not** in the mud!

Tug the bus, Tib!

Bec had a job for Tib.

The ram is in her dam!

Tib can get the ram.

Tib can tug the ram.

Tug, tug, tug ...

The ram is not in the dam!

Tib did jobs for Dan
and Bec.

Tib got the bus and the ram.

Tib was not sad.

Tib had fun!

CHECKING FOR MEANING

1. Why is Tib sad at the start of the story? *(Literal)*

2. Tib can not dig, but what can he do? *(Literal)*

3. How do you think the ram got stuck in the dam? *(Inferential)*

EXTENDING VOCABULARY

sad	Say the sounds in the word *sad*. Take away the letter *s* and put another letter at the start to make a new word. How many different words can you make?
get	How many sounds are in the word *get*? What are they? If you change the *e* to an *o*, what is the new word? Can you use the words *get* and *got* in sentences to show their meanings?
tug	What is another word that means the same as *tug*? Which words do you know that rhyme with *tug*?

MOVING BEYOND THE TEXT

1. What type of vehicle is Tib?

2. What is another job Tib could do?

3. Do you think Tib likes his job? Why?

4. What jobs do you think Gus the bus might do?

SPEED SOUNDS

Dd	Jj	Oo	Gg	Uu

Cc	Bb	Rr	Ee	Ff	Hh	Nn

Mm	Ss	Aa	Pp	Ii	Tt

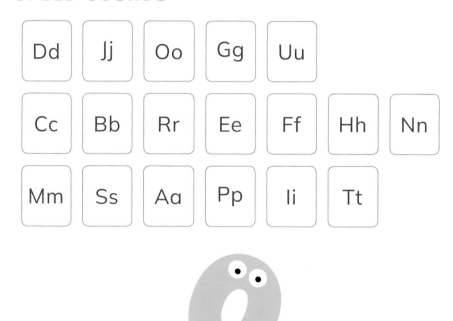

PRACTICE WORDS

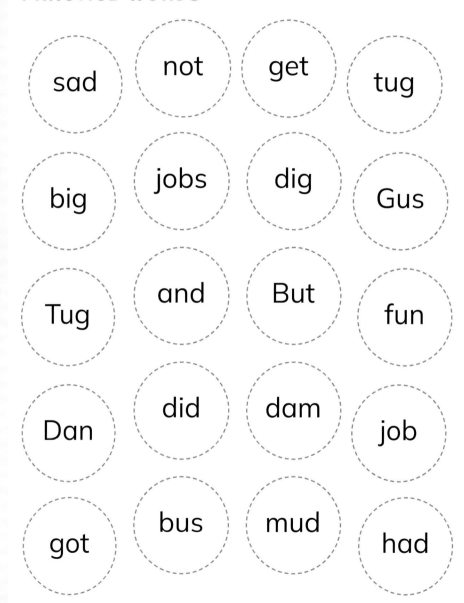

sad

not

get

tug

big

jobs

dig

Gus

Tug

and

But

fun

Dan

did

dam

job

got

bus

mud

had